FEARLESS EXPRESSIONS:

A TIME FOR US

By BoYenhwa

Plain & Simple Books
North Bend, Oregon

Fearless Expressions / Bo Yenhwa

Plain & Simple Books, North Bend, Oregon
ISBN: 978-1466236684
Copyright September 2011 by Bo Yenhwa
Library of Congress Control Number: 2011936687
Manufactured in the United States of America
10 9 8 7 6 5 4 3 2 1

Dedication

To the love of my life; my loving and supportive husband, David Zucker

"Writing is not a source of pain.
It's psychic chemotherapy.

It reduces your psychological tumors
and relieves your pain!"

~Dean Zoontz

Table of Contents

"Religion is for people afraid of going to hell,
spirituality is for people who have already been there."

~Anonymous

Reflections through Broken Mirrors

Broken Wing

i sang a song so pure, so true,

soar into the sky bright blue

when disrupting my path again, you flew.

Zig-zagging, squawking, flapping-

distorting my view.

So i slowed right down and let you through.

This yielding act, you thought untrue.

Perplexed, unsure just what to do-

maybe scared, angry or blue

when you ripped my wings apart in two.

Bits and pieces in the wind they blew.

Side to side i wavered and in lieu

of all that i've been taught, i knew

there was not much that i could do.

So naive & without a clue,

i fell so fast-

panic- blast.

Oh damn, here comes the ground!

Oh no, it's the long island sound!

i landed in a crash,

came up to the surface

with a splash.

And then i knew.

i was a survivor-

through and though.

made it out alive- true blue.

So i sang again

a song so pure, so true-

soar up into the sky bright blue!

Reactions to Bells

Living hell is an empty shell.

Living well is a destiny bell.

Ring.

Ring.

You hear it and maybe

even choose to sing.

You'll have a good day

and be on your merry way.

Ring.

Ring.

You hear it and this time

choose to sting.

Like a jump start to a motor,

this trigger's relentless.

You've hurt someone now,

rejected-

denied-

dismissed-

the ringing of a bell, true bliss.

Now when this is the choice you make,

beware of karma for goodness sake.

Ring.

Ring.

Responding too quick

could end you up sick.

But blessings are fragments of time in disguise.

Only thing holding us back is our bitter cold lies.

welcomed-

secured-

relaxed-

Finally, time to unwind and just crash.

Lay out on that tattered old chair.

Ponder, sit and make a wish,

until you find, sweet serenity and real true bliss.

11

Contagious

They are chasing me, still, I am tired.

As I walk down charter street,

all I see are monsters,

engulfed in rage.

Uncontrollable.

The desire to keep running is fading.

Stumbling down the steps, my legs shake.

It feels like I've been running all year.

fighting these zombies-

their power intoxicating, I'm enraptured with fear

and for a moment I almost give in.

Maybe it wouldn't be so bad,

living with the dead.

overcome by my weariness,

they draw me closer.

Frightened and excited,

simultaneously.

Oh no! Too late!

I'm fading now.

I'm done.

I stop dead in my tracks-

their breath on my neck,

they've already won.

Their blood and mine are one.

New Life

I woke up earlier than I thought on that blessed day!

Beauty unraveled-

one by one-

piece by piece...

As the images surrounded me with tidings of   comfort.

Snap! Snap!

The camera lens chats.

Inhale one, two, three...

Let it out. Exhale.

Warm, white and radiant light pulses up my spine.

A tear trickles down-

for no apparent reason.

All I know is, I don't know-

the allure is in the season.

To feel is to be alive-

these emotions, so raw, like a newborn child.

I am starting to see the world for the first time-

in a new light.

Accepting, understanding and gentle to myself,

I am ready to start a new life.

Out in the Crowd

Oh how I wish I were invisible.

Not in that pathetic way people feel

when their pain is too apparent

it floods the room with despair.

No, not that kind.

Just in the maddening recesses of my mind-

comes out in the quiet times

like at church.

In a library.

Waiting in a line to purchase.

It's like I want to scream and shout!

Dance on the tables-

just to pout.

Or when someone slams words down,

I think may be wack-

turns my stomach inside-out.

But societal chains keep pullin' me back.

There ain't no way for these word are like led.

Heavy inside and they'd rather zone out and be like

they're dead.

What if we shake them from the inside?

Wake up shallow drones-

listen to a new hope-

true wisdom won't come from that pope.

Blind love is real in the literal sense,

but to be blinded by faith should be a federal offense.

Guided by the Sheppard who walks in the night,

he never loses tract of the shinning bright light.

Close your eyes and the world you know

disappears.

Stillness is the only comfort you fear.

Why?

Maybe if you were invisible you'd know.

Or blind? Or deaf? Or mute?

Or maybe all you need to do is listen.

Listen to the unspoken words that bring your eyes to tear.

Wonder what that toddler felt

when she held tight

to her first real doll.

Bitter lies can hold truths in disguise-

while sins will lead us to our final demise.

Traveling down that same dusty road

until one day you find it's been over paved-

where her name was engraved.

In glorious songs from a dove-

and beautiful surprises,

you're in love.

What a journey &

you've only just begun!

Let's dance-

Let's laugh-

while under the sun!

All those years wasted-

in more ways than one.

So much work to be done!

Oh to be the invisible one-

hard-headed.

Spunky.

And misunderstood.

Quiet.

Or grim.

None of this would

matter-

Alone off the grid.

18

Manic

Head spinning like the top toy my baby niece picked up.

Is this how my mind picks up waves and radio sounds?

All distorted and contorted-

without a piece of solid ground to stand.

Perspectives ring true through my cognitive jukebox.

Only, I'm outta spare change and even if I did-

would it even matter?

I think it's out of order and probably shattered.

It plays whatever song it feels-

no control, it's on its own beat.

Like my head, there no retreat.

like a game of tennis-

it's the double edge sword.

My refuge, my pleasure, my pain.

But what is there left to gain?

The ball bounces back and fourth

until one of us tires out.

It's manic solitary bliss,

will keep us locked into this abyss.

<u>Broken</u>

I'm broke again like a' $5.00 swatch.

I don't know the time cause my face's all bubbly-

absorbed in too much water suddenly.

This is how I feel when I can't rest easy.

I blow you a kiss from my castle in the sky,

while tears drip from the cornea of my eyes

and all I see is fuzzy and glossy.

I am staring into the abyss.

Wake me!

Help me!

Shake me!

I broke again and the pieces just don't fit.

The knowledge of the detrimental

despair and agony which awaits me,

when my mental castle disappears

is haunting.

But there's nothing I can do,

the task's too daunting.

Forget it!

Save it for another day,

when I'm awaken by the sun's ray.

The Masks we Wear

Blind passenger, Blind faith...

Behind the mask your fate awaits.

The dark mask was creeping in,

drawing closer as I fell.

Hiding from the sun's warm light,

only made my mask fit tight.

Was it the lips that deceived me?

Or your eyes?

It's hard to see the man inside,

when you're inside out and backwards too.

RoyGBIV are the colors of the rainbow,

but at a glance, just nonsense.

The dark passenger has been

there all the while-

Shadow partner,

your friend.

A permanent lover,

kept under cover.

The clay has hardened.

Layers upon layers of lies.

The bitter disguise,

with us always till our demise.

Through her dry and flaky skin-

decrepit and old,

a fresh new shade of youth unveils.

As a chrysalis awaiting its bloom,

beauties humble nature

is coming soon

to a forest near you,

as she steps out of the shade-

her vision's come true.

<u>Kaleidoscope</u>

Colors illuminate my world,

when I'm here.

Easy to forget-

when drowning in regret.

Misery has left me blind.

Blind to the rainbows & gardens.

Fear found my mind when I lost it.

Wrapped its insidious noose around my neck.

What on earth was I doing that couldn't distract me enough

to forget?

Slipped down that slippery slope.

When this happens it's easy to lose hope.

Children are beacons of lights & inspiration.

Thank god for all this insight-

only possible to see by

the kaleidoscopes in flight.

The Nothing

The nothing is coming for you.

It's here for one sole purpose;

to shut you off,

keep you far away

and spin you around

so fast you won't even see the ground.

The nothing will turn your world upside down;

taking control of your soul.

Your ego rules now and there's no going back,

unless you decide to get on the right track.

Letting go of your mind may at the moment feel right,

but it won't be long now till you give in to the fight.

Paranoia and fear creep in languidly,

as you begin to doubt the light,

that which had brought you here at birth.

When darkness intrigues the curiosity of earth,

the mysterious works of the nothing

reigns through hypnotic, ominous art.

Remember how much you love to love?

and the comfort of being alive, joyous and free?

Free, if you will, to do as you please.

Never let "nothing" make you fall to your knees!

Awaken the eyes that fool you.

Break the solitude which confines you.

Take off the blindfold and see the light.

No more will you let the *nothing* control you-

beyond hope and light;

night

after

night.

Pepper-Spray

Booze and cheap cologne fill the air.

Greasy, wet, dirty-blond hair

so tangled and beer sticky,

still couldn't mask his dank breath of whiskey.

She thought you a friend,

but found out instead-

you contrived up a false bravado.

Thought you were some kind of desperado.

But all you were was desperate.

"You poisoned me-

and made me think I just got sick drunk.

And man oh man what horrible luck.

But no wonder why I was such a two beer queer that night.

I knew you were there on top of me when struggled to fight.

But that was like trying to walk through mud or glue.

It wasn't until the next morning, when I came to

that I figured out just what you did.

pepper spray would have been useful that night."

Too much

Too much,

today.

Too tired,

to pray.

My hands still feel dirty.

I drove right over a raccoon today.

Too sad,

today.

Too fast,

two cars drove on past.

Too soon,

today.

Too shocking

to be true.

Too achy,

tonight.

Too shaky-

my body shivers.

I drove over a raccoon today.

Two tears,

they trickle down my cheeks.

Too tender to disguise.

Too much,

today.

It's time to pray.

Addictions

Expired Trinkets

Death follows-

right behind you.

Tip-toes

He's creepin'

Spy when he must.

You might even be sleepin.

Gleaming

He's knowin

You fell and are stuck.

Even the tough outta luck.

As your pain gets deeper,

out steps the reaper.

Into your dreams he settles you,

so unclear, wallowing-

denying our fear.

Haunting and taunting-

he's lurking

he's stalking

Don't listen if he comes a knockin'!

You hum those sweet prayers,

those nursery rhymes

and anything peaceful to pass the time.

This distraction might work for a minute or two-

but what now should you do

when your senses are triggered

to the drug's sweet intoxication,

speaking straight to your disease-

bringing you down to your knees?

You ain't goin' on no airplane, train, or bus.

So there's no need to rush,

'cause this ain't no ticket-

the only road it leads to is nowhere.

So make these *expired trinkets!*

The Civil War

Addiction fits just like a glove

to keep up with the lies,

I just can't cope with out 'em.

Fucked up, yeah.

But stupid, nah.

Knowing this is half the battle.

"happily ever after"

only masked a lonely shadow,

now afraid and shaky- exposed for all to see.

Floating up and around the trees,

senses cloudy, mind's at ease.

What price will be paid off in the end?

The reaper is expecting you'll join the dead.

This civil war between lost souls-

will the fire ever leave them coals?

Ouch, burning and losing hope,

the pushers are smirking, claws on the dope.

High times are on the rise.

Beauty's the light she carries inside.

A tired, lost and dreary spirit

and darkness still holds on.

She feels it.

If only we could stop it!

Oh the masks we wear-

there's no escape-

smiles are ours to share.

So even when days feel like a civil war,

smile, laugh and be present with your God some more!

-With all life's empty promises and unexpected turns, it's only

fair-

and that's a triple doggie dare!

Sudden Darkness

Sudden darkness. Tears staining my existence,

smearing the mascara which shades my blackened eyes.

Reflection of fears, taking over souls.

One day you too will be told

The story that- which reflects your own.

Bitter and cold

Lonely and old

Lost and sold...

To the disease you carry.

Crack rocks scarcely scattered

Alone and battered.

The shame,

The humiliation.

F this game,

The degradation.

The blame.

Have you once again inhaled chalk fumes?

Perhaps popcorn, or some other crumbs in the room?

Coke smeared mirror reflecting the eyes of the

Beast.

They are mine, but not mine, for I am trapped.

He's come again, the haunting in my brain.

Running in the rain,

A vision of pain

Once again consumed with rage.

I keep turning corners but still in the cage.

Determined to go on, with my shadow to the cave of suicide, I hide.

Glorified, I'm on my honeymoon.

The engagement led to a marriage chained to fear and death.

I'm ugly inside.

But not to my disease.

"Come fuck me you princess,

take one of these,

it will bring you to your knees…"

I'm fuming inside.

But not to my disease.

"That's just the passion in your bones

and it tickles me."

I'm exposed

No longer composed.

Like an iguana froze.

In some ridiculous pose.

But not to my disease.

"You ain't no slut, you a free spirit.

Come on girl, do another line!"

Crushed, and now I'm spun.

This is not even fun.

Sudden Darkness.

I'm slipping-

Into the abyss of doom

Of a desolate room.

Tunnel vision and it feels so true.

There ain't no place for an addict who's blue.

Breathe...

Puff...

Toke...

Bluff...

Sing...

Dance...

Puff... Puff...

Alone in a daze

Shadows of footprints all over this maze

Still lost in the haze...

Sirens and shackles, how did this all happen?

Awaken my soul.

I don't wanna grow old.

Not like this.

Why?

Maybe I'll crawl up and die.

Drip, drip...

Sniff. Sniff...

Desperately I'm trying to hold on to that last dip.

There's no denying it now, I'm sinking,

and sinking quick!

The Haze

Drifting in and out of day dreams.

Constant reminders I am slipping.

When I fall, it's gonna hurt.

But I can't think like that -

It's time for work.

Writing in the dark,

fighting with my eyelids-

a funny thing,

but open they won't go...

Tight shut & for so long,

nothing changes

if nothing changes.

Literally, tired as I am,

I can't rest my head.

My lover has been tossin' & turnin',

refusing my tender love

that by now has turned stale.

Can I blame him?

Haunted tales & night sweats-

life sob stories with heads stuck in the sand.

Shadow Partner

Shadow partner, my friend.

Ace of spades, time to rewind.

Shadow partner, my friend,

always there in the end.

Where were you when your voice disappeared?

My mind shattered and I listened but could no longer hear.

In desperation, I ran from what I thought to be real.

Surrendering to the darkness that consumes me,

So no longer do I have to feel.

Gripping on too tight -

exposed and under *his* control.

Shadow partner, my friend,

always there in blood red.

Together we'll stand,

'till the bitter ends.

I may have left you, but I'll

never forget you.

When I was there, by your side.

You, shade so dark,

I became you.

Confused, I abused me who I thought was you.

Never again will I forget

shadow partner, my friend,

always there in my head.

Soma

Like a wrung out towel dripping water with every squeeze-

that is how my head feels on these "Soma-like" substances.

Sober and clean for some time now, but I can't escape the pressure.

The doc. keeps pushin' this chemically modified lifestyle-

but I'm dying inside and ready to quit.

This just ain't doin' the trick.

I'm numb downstairs-

lazy and scared

and all I see are shadows and cold stares.

This burnt out perfection seems pleasant at times-

yet its fuel has demolished my creative spine.

Now I can't even rhyme.

Like a lemon- I may look juicy, tasty, and even sassy-

but take a bite and you're filled with sour regret.

Take my word for it, "Somo's" no good for the gifted at heart.

Mess in the Mind

Words flow like water down the river,

with no rhyme

no reason.

Just to keep the hand going all season.

An enjoyable past-time for the easily dis-tractable victim in me.

This incurable disease

cancer cells attacking my will, sucking me dry

I let out a shallow, bitter cry.

So disparately I want to get high.

Unsure what will save me from my deepest fears -

the haunting memories of the last six years.

Chaos

I yearn for the darkest corners of my mind.

What the hell is wrong with me?

Am I losing my gratitude?

Forgetting the pain?

Consumed with resentments, I thought I'd left behind.

I need balance in my life.

The space between

me and myself is great

and I won't get where I want to be

if I tread by with backwards thinking

so I need to try

To live in the moment is blessed if you can

get out of your own head

and not wallow up and sulk instead.

It's obvious I'm not so, "Spiritually awakened" yet,

but at least my spirits not dead anymore.

Cuz when I was out there,

reaping the harvest that I sowed

I was at my bottomest low,

feeling jaded

about old friends still drinking, smokin' and tokin'.

Don't they see the insanity?

Do I miss the denial my addiction caused?

No, I'm grateful for this clarity

and for this recovery I've been sold.

-Hooked on the positivity I firmly hold.

The tools that were freely given to me,

a survival guide for the soul,

will finally fill that empty hole.

<u>Driftin and Zonin'</u>

I'm all alone again.

My disease haunts me.

"So what? Keep your head up! What you sulkin' for?

Just smoke some pot? Or hit up a rock?

Be grateful for all this new money you got! Let's get cocked!"

"I sure am... Gratefully God gave me these here eyes,

so I can shut you outta my sight.

Peace of mind is my new found delight-

these ears to silence you-

a beautiful clean mind to unravel you-

and drown you out with my own light.

Mind tricks of the Jedi come out in the night.

Slipper Slopes

Eyes on the dope

like quicksand pulling you faster-

the harder you struggle.

Whispers calling in the night,

now you are in trouble-

mesmerized by the light.

Lines packed tight

Glittering and bright.

No matter what you're told

remember they've already been sold.

The devil bought them long ago.

Let it go.

Cuz' it ain't no bargain,

even when it's free.

There's always a price,

when you're rollin' the dice.

Slippery Slopes

I'm about to choke.

50

Cough bitter fumes and

musty crite.

By dusk everything will be alright.

Wondering and lost,

I closed my mind,

uncertain what I might find

and how much it's gonna cost.

All I could do was bust out that night.

In the grip of the monster,

I fled the scene.

I'm not talkin' about the police,

but the man who had me on my knees.

Best thing to do was to take what he gave me

and snort it up fast.

I needed to feel that incoming blast.

Got me so jumpy I nearly crashed.

Now I needed something dopey

to quit feelin' this loopy.

Slippery slopes, in a bitter disguise
hustled in lies
and ransacked those naivety eyes.

Now was all dreamy in a hellish sphere
unveiled by a false heavenly tear.

What happened next was a blur
and all I could do was mutter and slur.
Thank God for detox.
I will never forget NA and new friends
who were there in the end.

In my death, I was reborn
& I'll never forget the God that
carried me and gave me a chance to breathe.

Angel's Breath

In the distant sky

you disappeared,

found somewhere to hide.

A great sadness

resounds

through my tear stained eyes.

Loss. Grief. Regret.

Help me! Please help me!

My ship is sinking and I'm barely hanging on.

Crying with the rain the tree brought in when

it fell.

Drowning in the flood that sunk

my house.

Guilt. Failure. Frustration.

We're sinking in the confusion

of things left behind...

things lost

and things found.

Fragments of Love

<u>Night Visions</u>

Fingers twitching, mouth humming.

Melodic phrases must be coming.

I can't help but peep.

Tossing and turning, he longs for sleep.

Gazing into his shut eyes I yearn-

wondering what desires between us will burn.

So many days and nights together,

still, I feel light as a goose feather.

Echoing voices reverberate through our bodies,

reminding us that all is impermanent,

yet all is so beautiful now, in its perfect align.

So relish in the spiritual divine

and keep your eyes open for incoming signs.

Stars Up in the Sky

When staring up at the sky, with you in my arms,

my one and only all star lover-

Tears fill my eyes

I can't help but to sigh.

Just wondering how I got so lucky,

and why?

Under the covers, my light discovered in the dark,

like that cool fresh breeze rushing through you at the park.

Or a warm embrace that's impossible to escape

when shivering swiftly by the ice cold lake.

When he is by my side, the power of our magnetism

cannot be described, broken or otherwise disrupted.

Gazing at the stars up in the sky

We contemplate

the question-

the ultimate-

WHY?

The Fire Starter

I am the fire starter

the trouble maker wakin'

rememberin' dreams, the old, the new-

the ones you have taken.

You stuck to me like glue

then up and left without a clue.

I knew not what to do.

but if you only knew...

I lit that match,

you flew

into my arms you crashed.

My mind plays tricks on me.

Wish you'd just let me be-

so I can do the same.

It's only just a game-

Still you had made me mad.

That dance that made us sad,

the night that thing went bad.

I hope you understand,

this fire starter's damned.

My Rock

Hitting nearly every bump in the road on the way to the ocean...

A humdinger! Thought I may have seen the singer of the sea...

I rose and saw the creature of the sea sitting upon a bundle of rocks.

Inhaling one breath, I ran across the ankle deep waves, and held it to my chest.

Imagining that this rock, my rock would be forever in a dream.

There I felt it- upon my fingers- tight in palms, but slipping...

My rock, poor, poor rock.

For he was full of life and now...

Chipping, chipping, chipping away....

Sand is all around me.

Water flows in between my toes and around my ankles.

Eyes fall shut when I throw back my head as my feet emerge, deeper into its grains.

Euphoric delight sings to me, beckoning me. "Stay... Stay..."

Stillness prevails over instinct to move,

kissing the air as if to thank it for rescuing me from my own despair.

My rock...

This rock...

God's rock...

Still chipping, and I am sinking...

Falling deeper and deeper within the grains of the protective sand.

Crustaceans are nibbling on my toes but I'm still sinking.

Your rock that once was solid, now is slipping...

I'm scared.

Lonely and feel so old.

It's cold.

I grip so hard onto my rock-

God's rock...

My gift from the creatures of the sea-

My song...

My solidity...

My sanctuary...

My grasp turns my knuckles pink

my hands white from holding on so strong-

And then, it happens.

Fragments of rock scrap my palms and etch through the skin under my nails.

Now, like pebbles they trickle down and all around me.

In an instant and like an escalator, I too move down faaaaast

61

Down...

Down...

Down...

Deep...

Deep...

Deep...

I might be running out of stock.

All because my stone rock.

Chipping...

Chipping... Chipping...

Chipping away and left me behind.

Left me with nothing

and everything at the same time.

I have been swallowed up within

the depth inside my mind!

Wake Up! Wake up!

Relief sweep! It was just a dream!

Choices

Breathe in the air.

Don't drown in your solitude.

Listen to the inner voice, and awaken you soul.

Freedom is found within.

A break through the ice.

A circle of friends, surrounded by darkness,

sheltered by light seems prophetic.

Strong is the magic that filled the luminous

moon on that misty night.

But all are illusions; refractions of light.

The shadows swallow our existence and

feed our addictions.

This is not a game or another prescription.

Wretched spirits trapped within the confounds

of their final resting place, unite.

So don't test them.

Live your life to the fullest,

but don't second guess them.

<u>May I?</u>

May I just be a part of your life?

A part that will bring a smile to your face?

I see you.

You see me.

Day after day we see

into each other's souls,

yet this never grows old.

Stay by my side when times are rough

and I promise, together we'll still remain tough.

I can't help the way I feel.

This knot in my stomach when you are near.

The love I have for you will always be so real.

So I ask you once again...

May I?

<u>Aching</u>

Gazing out this window, I'm aching,

inside, I am shaking.

I feel you are my everything,

yet you are only just an illusion.

Running through my head, you chose me.

Cutting like a knife,

you broke me.

Now, razor sharp and piercing,

you taunt me.

Watching and waiting,

you pace me,

Opening my heart as you chase me.

I'll be here, just obviating.

Gazing out this window, I'm falling.

Snap! like the loose branch I swung from as a child.

But I am all grown up now and this break

was not like the last.

I lost my grasp.

It's my final chance.

Slipping.

I'm slipping;

Falling through the cracks.

No one sees what I see.

No one hears my cries.

You are not here and without knowing what I'm waiting for,

How could you see my tears?

Gazing out this window, I'm on the brink.

Be gentle with my soul, for I am sure to sink.

Desire: Part I

I want a man to bring me flowers,

with glassy eyes upon the shadows.

Walk beside me.

No need to guide me.

Two hearts will diverge as one.

Awaiting for that morning sun.

Alone we sit, the three of us.

He looks deep within my soul.

I look back and softly speak.

No words, just talisman-like echoes of speech.

Our whimsical earth, so divine and pure.

We smile, breath and greet.

I sit and begin to meditate.

Now we three are one.

in awe of each other's presence we wait.

Patience is the virtue of love,

but so hard to keep those thoughts at bay.

Our answers will come when least expected

and maybe when the orange ball arises again,

the three of us will be once more!

<u>Desire: Part II</u>

"Open up, but not too fast! Slow down, you'll miss a vital glance.

You never will know when comes your final chance."

Worries as such one of ten come up

and then you ask *why?* to empty your cup.

It seems so obvious and trite, and in time,

you too will give up the fight.

Surrender all desires, attachments and possessions,

and I promise, you too will see, the universe's love for you

is oh so very, very real!

Intuition knows all but can be hard to bare.

For the truth will not always be so fair.

It's self-doubt and uncertainty that slides us

off the tracks of our destiny.

Simplify the mind and quiet the soul

and the man with flowers will be yours

two fold.

Fall from Grace

Oh my lover, don't you feel my suffering

Oh my lover don't you feel my pain.

Wait for me-

wait for me.

In here nothing

seems real.

But you know me-

You've shown me

just how to feel.

As rain falls-

then blood stains, on blue jeans.

Time stands still.

Let go of the pain that

consumes you.

I'm coming to rescue you.

When they bite the hand that feeds-

and they throw you in their solitude,

69

don't drown in the tears that fool.

No longer need you be their tool.

I know those dark clouds will lift away.

I'll shelter you like the warmth of a loaded gun.

I'm on my way and the gate may be closed,

just rest assure I'll find a way, I'll stay composed.

The fog from within your eyes-

will soon be the burden of his loss.

The lights on-

but nobody's home.

Answers are there-

buried hands in prayer.

The stillness around you,

like the desert at midnight-

has opened up for you

and the light in your eyes has filled the void,

inside our torn up souls.

Don't let it go...

All my innocence, lost in misery

Oh my lover, don't you fall from grace.

Wait for me-

wait for me.

In here nothing

seems real.

But you know me-

You've shown me...

just how to feel.

As rain falls-

then blood stains, on blue jeans.

Time stands still.

Let go of the pain that

consumes you...

My love for you has consoled me.

In the end, it will be our love that will save our light.

I'm coming for you through their castle tonight.

Drowning out the echoes of laughter

I'm swimming faster.

Can't wait to grasp you

and free you from the

chains that clasp you.

All my innocence, lost in misery

Oh my lover, don't you fall from grace.

Wait for me...

Wait for me...

Wait for me...

Unrequited Love

Where were you when my eyes were flooded?

Drowning in the tears of unanswered prayers.

I'm lost and confused but my love is true.

I wonder how I'll ever get next to you.

Is it love or is it lust?

I must admit, at times I forget.

we laugh.

we cry.

You look me straight within the eye.

Why then do we say goodbye?

my friend, turned lover,

wish we were not so undercover.

I want some sanity.

Don't tell me it's just games and vanity!

That's what I heard from a little bird,

but lust without love just seems absurd.

Freedom from Politics

Busy Bees

Busy bees.

Hustle bustle.

Shadow government's got us under a muzzle.

Sugar. Caffeine. Booze. Nicotine.

Jesus, we're not too far off from machines!

Enslaved to remain alert, focused and productive-

after all, fuck our health this is all for the sake of mass

consumption.

Wish I had something prophetic to say,

but the Soma they give, disrupts my creativity bay.

Until then, I'll be here maintaining our hive,

while the queen bee rests and hides.

They call it the "rat race"-

what a disgrace.

Good ol' US of A left long ago,

now divided, we stand-

working our tails off to feed *the man.*

Now we're in so much debt and turmoil,

we've lost our land.

We're brought down to our knees,

too distracted by Kayne West, Lady Gaga

and Black-Eyed Peas!

Question the Feed

So caught up inside the feed-

I think I forgot how to plant a seed.

Screamin', shoutin'

all day reactin'

makin' my ears bleepin' bleed.

Think it's too much?

Are you tired enough?

Sick of the arson's aching need?

Sick of stalkin', hauntin', tauntin'?

Facebook, I-Tunes, cyber games, email

Where and when?

Such a lonesome trail?

Campfires, home cookin' and scary ghost tales-

real rock heroes that didn't involve

a spaced out kid by the TV set-

cradling a placebo guitar

with multi-colored buttons

disguised as a fret?

Art shows, writing letters in fountain pen-

not typing all alone in the dingy old den?

Manual cameras and film in the park?

Developing pictures,

enjoying the mysterious room of the dark?

Picture hues manifesting so natural and true.

Now with "photo-shop" art,

little Johnny can tell you

just where to start.

So remember where you came from

next time, you're cruisin' the net,

'cause just ya never know when your

mind gets spent.!?

Question Everything

Question the girl who watches you eat,

for she may be fervid to consume you.

Question the man giving out thick wads of cash,

for he may be waiting to siege you.

Question the arms that hold you tight,

for they may be anxious to smother you.

Question the cohort always eager to please,

for he may be a snitch rat double crossin' stat cat.

Question the cabal who follows the crowd,

for they may be apt to harm those who do not concede.

Question the anti-conformist posse against the majority

because the anger may brew to an unending battle.

Question the proprietor who hires you,

for he may be thirsty for blood.

Question the one who reveals no secrets,

for they hold the ones jammed deep and usually most toxic.

Question those who talk too much,

for they maybe too damaged inside to listen.

Question those who diminish your pride,

for they may carry envy too heavy to hide.

Question the technology feed which links you in,

for it maybe only be days till it bleeds you dry.

Question the sanity of those who persecute and judge,

for they may be vengeful and full of oppressive rage.

Question the poet who writes this poem,

for she may be lost, damaged and confused.

Question all things in life because all is impermanent,

yet don't fear the unknown because we all are one

and eventually return to the original source.

Ponder that for a minute while when you diverge

from the comfort of your usual course.

Power Fuels the Hungry

As a shark would, he hunts his prey with

absolute certainty he *will* satisfy the ache

inside his rumbling belly.

Without a doubt...

Without fear...

Without hesitation...

he sinks his teeth in and devours his prey.

Empty Suits

They walk on by in their empty suits

eyes peeled safely on the loot.

Surrounded by shadows of the other,

lurking, quickly and under cover.

Heads held high and

ties tucked tightly like a noose.

The audience shivers, they're on the loose,

Underneath their children's shells-

using them as shields is a living hell.

Clouded by the breath of booze,

lies washed up dad in torn up shoes,

once again, to strum the blues.

83

A Walk

I went for a walk to clear my mind

while one hundred thoughts still lingered.

Not here.

Not there.

I breathe in the fresh air

And ponder on the fear and sadness deep within me

when I heard about the oil spill that demolished our beautiful
sea.

Life is no joke, and it's hard to let something so tragic just *be.*

I thought we were spared when I took

that final bow.

Little did I know, I was just a face in the crowd.

I pray to the Buddha as the corps roll the dice.

Maybe next time they'll think twice.

Who's next in this blame game?

They should be hanging their heads in shame!

But as I went on walking to clear my mind

while one-hundred thoughts still lingered.

<u>Hungry Ghosts</u>

Hungry ghosts are in our blood and also deep within the one,

two, three of you who dwell in one.

It's all too much- you're overjoyed and out of luck.

Feeling so empty-

the desire's unrelenting.

Our eyes are big,

Our throats are small,

and our belly, biggest of them all.

With throats so narrow and long,

the big, big tummy's never full.

Impossible to satisfy the ever present

and aching need to feed.

Obama Deception

The Obama deception...

Scary as hell-

to know there is no way out

when they ring the final bell.

We salivate, procreate, resuscitate...

Then scream and shout-

when we end up to our throats in dept

just where they want us,

barely able to breath-

but we march on,

Carrying the seed.

Gripping tight to our D&D mugs,

they twist and turn our proverbial wits

to lonely cries and irritating fits.

"America runs on Dunkin." They say.

The slogan rings true in so many ways...

Weaving in and out of a system where only the elite are in control.

But they got us hooked and most don't even know.

They dangle their carrots right under our noses.

Deception is easy when you know how to please.

Just get rid of the old village idiot president that nobody liked and replace him with the illusion of a polar extreme:

An intellectual, high-spirited, noble, young family man.

The first black man to become president of the good ole' US of A.

So exciting it was to hear about change-

Isn't this exactly what we've been waiting for years?

But the cryptic elite on their billion-dollar thrones know just what to say when they break another courageous spirit.

As soon as this man was elected-

Boom! Snatch! Watch out!

They must have told just what to do...

for Kennedy, Hoover and Kucinich knew.

If he doesn't listen they may have thrown in a threat or
two.

No one wants to get shot, crashed, or buried.

This man has a family to protect so of course

he'll rearrange what he said.

Wouldn't you too?

When if not, you'd end up, somehow dead?

I can't believe I fell, although many of us did.

Was it the change, the diversity, the elegant vernacular
arrangement of the pitch?

As they bask in their exploitative glory,

we march on to school, to work or to play-

Either way we turn, we're chained to this game.

Slurping up the muck, slopped into our bowls.

No way around it, sugar's on the rise!

Consumers beware, the *corps will keep us addicted-

Remember, no ethical laws to stand by or oppose.

Oh and just so you know,

they won't stop at obesity, diabetes or lung cancer to end the corruption of enslaving society-

especially now, when the population's rising high.

So just remember to kiss your kids goodbye.

Turn off the TV, Internet and shut out the news.

With all this in effect, you'll end up with the blues.

So take a walk with a friend and chill for a moment.

No need to worry about showing up two minutes late!

For this is our Karma too, our chance to meditate...

To reflect on the gifts that we've been givin' through faith.

Count your blessings.

We are in this together,

like birds of a feather.

Facebook: The Next Generation of Communication

It's a Facebook world for us.

It's a Facebook world for us.

'stead of kisses, we get texts

'stead of postcards, we get pics

It's a Facebook world!

Got the Motorola phone,

It's the techno- world we know.

Apple I-Pods

'stead of discs!

Three G Internet,

more debt.

It's a Facebook world!

Blogging seems to be the way.

We got icons, smiley face!

Spelling is a thing of the past.

Our nanites may us out last!

It's a Facebook world!

Digi-pets, lap tops, PlayStation!

Have we forgot how about penmanship!?

It's a Facebook world!

'stead of talking, we get chats.

'stead of visits, we get hits.

It's a Facebook world!

We navigate with GPS,

It's the Tivo digital.

Said he wants 10 gigs instead.

Now the chips inside his head.

It's a Facebook world!

Stories Retold

Tammy Rafaella Yurtle the Turtle

An hour drive later-

no make that two,

damn that traffic!

What more could we do?

A plump smelly girl and cigarette fumes.

One hundred and two lonesome country tunes,

three flights of stairs,

the kindness of stranger,

who turned out to be an old high school mate.

Another hour drive back home

and three coffee cups later,

a piercing shriek voice rang loud in my eardrum

showing and telling me just how to setup "Pedro's" tank

and believing every word, that was that;

she thanked me and off she went.

Ahhh. I can breathe. Just "Pedro" and I.

We rescued you from that disorderly house.

You poor thing.

All abandoned and cold.

I watched you for hours, like a stoner watching the Discovery channel.

You captivated and fascinated me.

And when that door slid open,

it startled me.

My fiancé was home so I ran right beside him,

grabbed his hand to lead him to our new found pet!

He froze in astonishment then said with regret,

"What were you thinking? This tank is a mess! Plus it's 55 gallons and this turtle's enormous!   You never told me you were saving a Galapagos!"

His anger was clear and I couldn't blame him.

He thought he was HAD, which then made him MAD-

so I told him it won't be all that bad!

We'll figure out something,

we'll have to, we must,

'cause I was HAD too.

I was told this boy, "Pedro" was small,

not 12 inches tall!

But when I saw that large tank all abandoned

in that cracked out old house, dirty water-

smelly and all-

I knew I had only a minute or two to decide.

I ran out of options.

it's too late now.

I was stuck.

'Cause I'm an animal lover,

flat outta luck.

But just when I thought,

"well, it won't be that bad..."

We find out through our research that every thing's wrong!!

1) The UV light was expired for a year or two- No UV makes it hard for digestion and calcium too!

2) The heat light for his rock was too weak a wattage.

3) The turtle had no heater for the cold water-

without heat, a cold-blooded creature can't really eat!

They're unable to actually produce heat!

4) The filter cartridges were a much different size

5) We needed more rocks

6) And on top of it all, due to this turtle's abuse and neglect for so long, he needed a medical kit to restore him to good health.

So we got all that stuff needed and spoiled him rotten, feeding him fish, crickets, veggies and shrimp.

Our wallets were empty we spent WAAAY over fifty.

The girl lied to us and refused to admit it later.

Left us high and dry, not a penny to spare.

The worst, maybe funniest of all,

was that this turtle, named Pedro, come to find out,

is not even a male...

She's a girl we could tell,

by the claws and the tail!

One last thing, before this story comes to an end.

This bitter, sad tale turns around in the end.

We renamed her, Tammy Rafaella Yurtle the Turtle.

Tammy- to make clear he's really a SHE

Rafaella- 'Cause we never liked the name "Pedro" and changed it
to Rafa short for Rafael

(like Nadal- our fav. tennis player)

Yurtle- 'Cause her kind has been around since the dinosaur age,
so we call her "wise" like Mack in the Dr Seuss book, "Yurtle, the
Turtle", calling her "Yurtle" for rhyming sake-

or if you prefer, perhaps the Chili Pepper's song!

Plus we found out these turtles live very, very long-

50 years or more and thank God they are such resilient
creatures,

because now she's the house's main attraction and feature!

Plus we were just recently told,

turtle's bring lots of good luck,

so we no longer feel like we were punked.

Thugs

Every day, on my way to school, lesson plans embraced with pride.

Turing the corner at double pace as usual-

eyes forced on pavementtracing the cracks.

Feeling their eyes weigh heavy, like magnets-

yet I stay focused on my destination.

Echoing taunts and Ebonic phrases followed close behind.

I was doing alright until I heard my name.

Senses engaged and like an electric shock

I'm triggered.

Lips and gums numbed.

Heart speeds up and I want to fly.

Leave it all behind.

Instead I move on faster.

Three years is not long enough to forget when I walked beside them.

Niantic

Sand-piper moves graceful upon the dome.

While we stagger out from our canoe and onto the ocean shore.

What appeared to be an oyster shell, whitened by the blazing sun-

was in truth, a sea bird's egg, cracked and empty-

left behind by some unknown predator.

I know this had to be,

because the sea bird eyed strong on me.

When I placed my fingers on the remnant of her unborn child.

Squawk! Squawk!

With a flap of her wings she was gone.

Hands in sand-

I ponder.

Knees buried; Body in prayer posture.

I pause and we wave goodbye.

The sandpiper let's out another wounded cry.

Locke, *The Tiger*

Once bitten, twice betrayed. Alone one day in his winter slumber
he had a dream; a long a persistent and troublesome dream.
Shattered were the memories that confined him to such a harsh
reality.

Despair, the vain but tender fool whose tender but bitter ideals
were sold to the darkness that winter brings to all the animals of
his kingdom of the divine where only a handful of such will rise
to truth such as he, the tiger did in that long winter's nap.

Him, the tiger,

Him, the beast.

Him, the tiger,

Him, the meek.

Entangled in his wretched twist, mind awoke upon then he
spoke, words all jumbled, for this was *his* dream; His hope, His
lead.

*"You all have worth, come hither and trust these words not mine,
but his words, that creature in the sky who knows the answer to all
the whys? Only will never tell, for it is us that must see. Be wise, be
forsaken even he was at a time, when living a lye. A disguise if you
must. Listen, now for there is danger upon us this ominous winter
and we must follow with our hearts and not just our primate
instincts because today, we, the animals, the gifts of the earth must
help the human race to see, we must use the part of our minds
unknown to the man. Please understand...."*

Interrupted, "Oh come on now! What's all this mean, anyhow? Worthy? Wise?" Shouted the rabbit beyond the bush. "I need to rest, its cold out there."

"A disguise? Foresaken?" The turtle asked in a monotone hush. "I'm sleepy too and live in my shell, protected from harm and I like it that way."

"Yeah, what's that you say?" The squirrel replied as he gathered more nuts and ran into a tree. "We are doing just fine and enough is enough. I've gathered my nuts and my families good, so please leave us alone you babbling glut!"

And before the tiger had time to respond a graceful young fawn approached him with wonder and awe. "My mother's not far and I am not supposed to talk to tigers, but..." she whispered, "What you say is intriguing and quite appealing. Go on...."

"No, no, no!" Chimed in the foul old skunk, "Danger, Daaannger, beware of this odd speaking creature. He is just here to entice you then eat you my dear!"

The little fawn gasped and ran off to the wood and the voices continued, all scattered about, chatting about this and that. No matter how much Locke tried, they would not listen, would not even try.

Sadly, he turned away from the crowd, tail dragging behind. He buried his head under his paws amidst some tall grass and the sun shone brightly, for in this dream he felt so free from winter's despair and hoped and prayed with all his might to find a way to reach them maybe later, maybe tonight!

As the sun set down low and the shadows cast, turned into a moonlight reflection and stars shinning bright, a large barn owl flew down on a low branch to perch, startling the tiger, still lost in his thoughts and rehearsing what he might say to his family, the creatures of the woods tonight.

"You, whoooo! You, Whoooo!" The owl said to Locke the Tiger, so alone that night. Locke looked up and felt relief, for maybe there was a friend left in the woods still for him. "They animals in these woods are much too young. The growth you seek in them is too much to hold. But please, stand strong, we are the two oldest souls and in time they will see, don't you worry, you whooo, you whooo!"

Locke stared up at the owl and asked, "Old souls, what do you mean?"

"Just that we have been around many lifetimes and no much, but the other will too, just not so soon.

Give it time, give it time and they too will grow."

And if shared by thoughts, they needed no longer speak. Thoughts were transparent and went back and

fourth without effort.

'Respect has not been earned yet, but will be in time.

Denial has flourished.

Ignorance won.

Wisdom and truth still unseen....'

On and on the owl and the tiger exchanged thoughts without words in the bizarre twisted dream.

103

Then the tiger went back to is den of solitude to ponder. In fact, there he stayed, the only one awake in mind but sleeping in the body of nature's beast, until spring, when the blooming for daisies and daffodils sang to him.

Him, the tiger.

Him, the wild.

Him, the beast.

For this is how the creatures of the forest saw him. Behind those eyes so deep so brown so large, they froze when their eyes cast upon him. He wondered if it was fear or curiosity that made them act this way. And often wondered if he would reach just one of them someday.

He was the animals scurrying about, playing and hunting and resting. But all were happy, all were well.

He awake briefly, and looked around at the barren, desolate grounds.

He shed a tear, remembering that none of this was real.

For in these sacred woods, year 2025, The three hundred and seven trees left provide us oxygen- just enough to breath, but more killing is occurring for greed has taken over the man's bitter soul. For it was he that destroyed the earth and did not know just what to do, so few, so few survived. Their brains slightly damaged due to toxic pollutant fumes. The younger you were, the worse it was for you and the virus took over quick. No tolerance for the estranged and minds as empty as an anorexic's dinner plate.

104

The virus of the soul, so toxic, leaving us empty and many fumed with rage. But a handful stood up and tried to protect the woods and all who lived among them. Those with no fear, no memory, only instinct and wisdom survived but many lost hope, lost passion and lost faith, only because they would not listen to the owl and the tiger. It was too much for them to grasp. Too painful to listen, in fear they will miss a meal, a hunt a game. Food scarce, muscles weak, the strong defeated the week and the wise hibernated as long as they could bear, no longer capable to seek. They had not worked together and that was what tore them so deeply apart, if only they could listen to the tiger's gentle thoughts.

Him, the Tiger.

Him, the brave.

Him, the lover of the rain

will soon return, rest assure of that my friend.

He woke today and told me so.

Happy Feet and Earth Vines

If these vines could talk,

I wonder if they'd share their tales.

Around the fence that shelters our sanctuary hide-

away buds begin to blossom in that all so beauty never,

never

never land.

The wind has kissed our cheek so many peaceful after noon,

while soaking up those alluring UV ray.

So many unexpected splashes from the youth in bare feet,

three feet tall,

forgetting all the rules.

No one seemed to mind these moments,

too blissful to disrupt such tiny happy feet.

He slurps up some A1 sauce that dribbles to the floor and then

<kurplunk>

a wad of meat lands so swiftly

lands right by the puppy's two front paws.

Making him lick his lips as he

cherished in every sloppy bite.

Close by, a lady, dressed in blue,

eyes shaded by her desert hat

reminded her happy feet to

be careful

when she eats

and to hold her plate up straight.

A drum beat sounds and mics are checked

as the others chat and stuff their face with fat.

As my leaves drift over the wooden shelter wall,

I think they call a fence-

happy feet munch-kins

and tired big creatures make their way over to the corner

where my buds are sprouting,

so close to tent.

Would she tell about our midnight kisses down

by the pool?

Can she see us as we stack the tables with her cousin's remains,

now transformed into plates and napkins.

Over abundance and careless actions subconsciously

embedded in our thinking muscle-

What we call the brain.

Graceful moments from her fragile vines

so thin.

107

I think I heard her whisper.

I turn my head and glance her way

reflecting on previous existing

ponders.

What happened next was

not believable-

But I'll tell you anyway.

An echo of my thoughts had traveled through

my ears.

It has been a year since that unforgotten dream-

safe in our hideaway.

B*R*A*I*N, brain,

my little friend with oh so

happy feet-

now grown and never to be forgotten.

But what is it that worries her

so much about these

P*L*A*T*E, plates

she won't to me explain.

Said I would not understand.

Touching with her tender hands,

my earthy vines,

she wishes in her mind

she didn't have such trouble in her

B*R*A*I*N, brain.

These happy feet and earth vines,

come out only in the rain.

Tales of Engagement

The First Proposal: A bit rushed and unprepared...

Sitting at a bar,

drinking a lager.

It was only an hour or two ago when we picked out the ring.

Together we planned it...

Together we ran with it...

Emotions running wild.

Many drinks were swallowed.

I knew it would happen sooner than later

Because he knew I was waiting and waiting.

Anticipation grew.

So just about when we were feeling quite buzzed,

his grin lit up as he shifted and stuttered,

face turning bright red,

he went on and said,

"You have been my friend through thick and thin.

I want us to be together until the end of time.

So, lady, my love, will you be mine?"

His hand from his pocket he pulled out the ring.

So happy I was, I wanted to sing!

I said yes of course and we kissed.

The bar folks clapped and an old man laughed.

The sexy bartender gave us a wink and smiled, "Congrats!"

But it was the two women lovers who came out from their cover,

to tell us how happy they were to discover-

we were sharing this joy with one another.

They were so happy, they even gave us their number

We planned on meeting up sometime for supper,

but lost it by the time we sought it.

The Second Proposal: _A surprise in the woods_

A year later and half way through our wedding plan

We are on our trail, out for a morning stroll.

It's Christmas eve and he announces,

"I have to pee."

So I walked down to the river and found a rock.

There I sat and gazed upon the rising sun.

At this time all was quiet,

my mind at ease.

Rustling of leaves, he is moving fast.

I plan on asking him to sit with me a while and relax.

Instead he says he thinks he found a turtle

but was not sure.

"I'm sure it's just a rock" I said with a wave.

"No, no, I don't think so! Come on, you gotta see!" He insisted.

With a sigh I reluctantly followed.

"There's no turtles around now silly. It's the dead of winter!"

But I was curious what it was he saw.

When he pointed I thought he was afraid.

So I laughed and stepped ahead,

when what to my wondering eyes should appear...

A little gift box with an "A" on the top, just for me.

More than surprised, I was shocked-

my, oh my...

Was going to propose again now that we're sober and true?

As I unwrapped and said how he didn't have to do this,

I noticed a letter all creased inside.

I opened the letter and within it was said with words

passionate and true, how special I was and

how much he admires my passion to teach and help people.

He spoke about how life was grand being in love with his best
friend was never planned,

and how much he would like to share a life together forever.

Among many other exquisite words from the heart,

he asked me again, "Will you be my wife?"

My body felt radiant and light.

I was so filled up with delight,

all I could do was giggle and cry.

Yes, a few tears were shed

and I held his hand in mine.

I kept saying over and over how much I loved him

and felt the same way too

when he had to stop me and ask again,

"Well, will you?"

I laughed and so did he because he knew what I'd say.

"Yes of course honey bear, I do, I do, I do!"

113

"Well open your present already!"

I unwrapped and saw that the little box was from a store called,

'Getting Off'

and abruptly I frowned and shot him a quizzical look.

He said it was not what I thought and just open it up...

So one brow raised up and a smile sprouting,

when I saw it, boy, my smile did grow!

It was a dragonfly necklace with opal wings

to match my engagement ring!

"I love it! Thank you!"

and all that jazz as we walked, cuddled and chatted some more.

We praised each other for our strength

through this sober awakening year.

And many more to come...

Our Wedding

A beautiful union of not just a new matrimony of husband and wife-

but of friends and families coming together a berry mix smoothie! Yum!

What a joy to celebrate our devotion to each other with such beautiful people.

We are truly blessed.

With just a sprinkle of hope, a dash of faith and a whole lot of love,

we will flourish and grow together-

forever and ever,

in the dharma, the sanga and with the Buddha's love.

<u>Our Honeymoon</u>

An escape to paradise!

Through the city of Waikiki,

zigzagging around hundred's of shopping centers and malls,

we made our way to the beautiful beach.

Waves calling out to us-

but we are in a rush.

Off to our next destination, five full days in Molokai!

A drive across the island, won't take much more than a couple of hours

and we stopped at so many places to snorkel, it didn't even matter.

A coffee plantation, a few tourist shops, grocery shop, one hotel, one resort and that's that.

The most remote spot,

so we swam quite a lot.

Oh and I can't forget the fish and dive shop.

We bought tickets to dive with the crew

and when we entered the boats we knew...

We were the only ones on that gorgeous Friday.

We swam with sea turtles, exotic fish,

and even saw spinner dolphins playing along side our boat.

What a sight-

all day long I could gloat

about our visit to Honolulu, Oahu and Maui too-

but that may be too long for a poem,

so I'll leave the mystery to you.

Recovery

A Prayer and a Blessing:
To Free the Angel, Trapped in an Addict's Withered Body...

May your will be thine.

May your truth be known.

Enlighten us with honor

and the value of respect.

May your universe

become our only craving

when the days get long and lazy.

May you open up our minds

to a the peaceful kind-

to nature, beauty and balance

that once we left behind.

The gift of giving-

from your cup to mine

keeps us living with the divine.

So selflessly, as you wade in our sea

of unfulfilled desires feeding on our misery-

you wipe each and every tear

take away all our fears.

Yet when we walk out in the dark-

not conscious of the warmth you spark

we disrupt that very moment.

The safety that you've given me,

please don't let me forget,

for if I do things *my own way-*

I know I'll have regrets.

This thing called faith

you've helped me perceive

will never, ever leave.

That is why I know I trust

this joy I truly *feel.*

This flowing light-it must be real 'cause I've given up the fight.

You gave us eyes to see

and so we let it be.

You gave us ears to listen

and so now we heard.

Now I pray for understanding-

guidance and your word.

I now declare, for all to hear that I am

willing to be blessed

and turn my will to you oh Lord,

because you are the best!

I am grateful for recovery,

because now I finally see.

You've intervened,

I don't know how-

but I've accepted anyhow.

122

This is where I'm meant to be.

<u>Doubts</u>

I used to be fearless.

Now, I'm having second thoughts,

starting to have doubts.

I'm powerless.

Peeps talkin' bout how great they feel,

when I still can't figure out

if any of this is real.

The blessing and curse of a new recovery-

has left me burning with a mind-numbing discovery.

Same old phrases.

Voices echoing,

"You go back & you'll be pushin' up daisies!"

"Alive, joyous & free"-

and if you're a newcomer,

"Just be patient, wait for the miracle!"

Sharing the same old shit,

gets mundane, sometimes I wanna quit.

Bored as fuck,

sometimes you wanna take a hit.

"Drop the ego"-

"No war stories"-

&

"Glorifying drugs is illegal."

This group may seem trite and even cultist at times,

day after day,

sharin' the same old rhymes.

Yet, with the friendships I have made,

I wouldn't want it any other way!

'Cause in the morning, I must admit,

I'm so relieved I don't need some kind of fix.

I hear the neighbors puking

and it makes me sick.

Brings me back to the days of the drink.

I used to be a walking mess,

125

hilarious.

Yet sometimes at my own expense.

What a thrill just to exist.

I hear them laugh,

and then a crash.

But me, I am a sober freak.

Fragile, clean and sheik.

The Lure of an Empty Paradise

My eyes opened for the first time when I broke free from the
chains that weighed down my soul.

So heavy, I gave up the struggle long ago, but my angels saved
me.

Broke me out of my trance - So I didn't take a second glance.

Just accepted it and went about my way.

Sweet nectar once called softly...

Bringing me into the lion's den.

Whispering pleasant sounds of nothingness,

entrancing me...

enticing me...

Curiosity and desire reverberated throughout my body.

So I followed - obediently.

blindly.

Like the greyhound chasing the rabbit, just to oblige to my
assigned role.

This disease took over long ago when I first became under their
control.

Although some days I feel like a space lady in the body of a
human.

skin itching for freedom, comfort and control.

I know that if I stay in today, my wings will grow.

In time it will happen- the day I fly.

May patience bestow upon me today and

every day as we blossom and grow...

leaving the empty paradise.

<u>Well-Being</u>

When you're feeling sad and blue and someone says aloud to you,

"Have a drink, relax."

That oxymoron phrase you hear so often

You must beware

Don't play the fool,

You've been to school.

You know the rules

And what will happen if you use.

No matter what the ads portray,

It doesn't have to be that way.

That's just misery seeking out company.

Don't open that cut, your wounds are healing.

And the fog is clearing.

A higher power marks the final hour,

not the pills, the liquor or poison flower.

Tick, Tock, there goes the analog clock.

To be well is to see through the spell.

The mind plays tricks in the head,

But if you listen, you could end up dead!

In protest the reluctant addict sighs,

"It's alright guys, I promise no more lies. I don't need help."

Frustrated friends and a fueled up families-

just give it some time.

Pray for the suffering. Look up to the night's clear sky.

Reminded of the torment that haunted my well-being

at a time when I didn't bother with the "whys?"

In this vast karma "*samsara*" universe,

being given the gift of recovery,

sometimes I wonder how long this will this last?

Or will one day bring me back to the curse of the past?

The rain may be gone, but on lives the haunting pain-

to remind us of yesterday's history.

It has been said,

"Yesterday's history

Tomorrow's a mystery, so enjoy today,

for it is a gift; that's why we call it the present." (Babatunde
Olatunji)

I wouldn't want it any other way.

We unwrap new gifts each day.

Inside them we find a piece of the sky.

So beautiful it will make you cry...

130

Bliss such like this should never be missed.

Packed down deep within the remnant of perpetual glory

depicts portions of *Life* and this never-ending story.

We write it down now through inspiration shared with one and other-

in these glorious days of truth and discovery.

Ignorant Lips found Wisdom and Wit

Euphoric sensation between my lips,

sweet Mary-Jane...

but from your bliss I must refrain.

For next comes the bottle, and then the cocaine.

Opiates follow to ease the pain.

There goes my dignity

right down the drain.

The rugs been pulled out from under my feet.

Can I complain that I no longer sleep?

Coming down's a bitch

Got that unwavering itch!

Lost my mind the day I continued to use.

Eyes blinded again by those shadowy hues.

Avoiding that God awful pitiful news.

What was there left for an addict to lose?

Shut out the world -

Pushed human contact away.

The drugs were my God and I liked it that way.

Why couldn't I stop? I may never know.

As long as I always continue to grow.

Thinking back on the past

I wonder how long this affliction will last?

With my hubby in the sack I get shivers down my back

reflecting on the person I used to be.

A liar, a cheat, inside was too ugly to see.

Last year at this time I'd be lookin' to cop.

Now all I can do is run around and shop.

It's so quiet on the outside, you can hear a pin drop.

But inside my head, thoughts all jumbled

like little itty-bitty pieces of led.

Back and forth they go like a ping-pong show.

But I'd take this state any day,

over a substance numbed alternative way.

<u>Surrender</u>

The life you live

are the paths you choose.

Be wise.

Don't forget, neglect or hide.

Stay bound tightly to the roots of the earth,

your mother, your past.

Yet give yourself the courage and motivation

to recognize the difference between the roots of the earth

and the roots of societal chains.

Travel the globe

and don't be a slave for money.

Work hard and with love in your heart,

but don't be a doormat,

for, your mind is strong.

Oppression is everywhere still.

Surrendering to a god of your understanding is the only escape-

so be humble.

Be wise.

Be kind.

Look at your life, your future and rewind.

Forgive yourself and live in the now.

This may be your last chance to be found.

Don't let these words be missed,

and he will reward you

with purity and bliss!

<u>On the Other Side</u>

Behind thick walls among empty faces and cold stares

I can only avert by casting my glare.

"Stay away dumpster divers. I ain't like you, and if you touch me,
it might just fuel me up enough to pile drive you!"

Sudden darkness- my disease screams at me

Turning on me in every way.

Cursing me...

Teasing me...

Haunting me...

"You stupid slut, what were you thinking?

Getting caught so fast!

You broke the rules,

You know better than that!"

My insides are turning, sweat drips from my forehead

I'm burning.

Cold and tired, hurt and cryin.

"But it was *you* who told me we needed more.

It was *you* that said I should steal from the store.

So why?

Why?

136

Why?"

More mascara trailed tears stain my skin.

Then I hear it.

Words that reflect my soul.

I swear they must be my own.

But no, this voice is hoarse, confident and wise.

The *me* I might have been without the disguise.

The past she shares...

The regrets she speaks of...

The fears she's lost...

I begin to wonder how?

These were my fears.

My regrets.

My LIFE!

Only this was my life now-

Her past.

How did she make it a thing of the past?

It felt good to pretend to be her, mind clear, open and free.

Chains of addictions at bay.

I turn the corner and peek inside.

A room full of addicts! Just like me!!

The darkness has faded,

A new light has entered.

Dawn is upon us.

My disease has quieted.

I can't even hear it and in the moment

I freeze to enjoy the blissful serenity.
This woman's voice is powerful.

She speaks with intonation and inspiration.

When she speaks,

I hear it.

Visions echoed through her eyes.

Through her lips she tells my life, my secrets, my lies.

It's my story in *her.*

A new found glory,

she gives me hope.

<u>Angels in the Rooms</u>

Where did they all come from?

They came from the darkness I used to dwell.

Who are they?

They are addicts, just like me.

In the grips of a cunning disease-

We live to use and use to live.

Why are they here?

For the same reasons I am:

To seek help, recovery, friendship and a loving God.

Is this a cult?

If we are – it's not like we're sacrificing animals or torching
people.

It is however possible that we are being brainwashed

by other addicts who created these steps to help each other stay
clean.

According to the Webster's dictionary which states that,

"a particular system of religious worship especially

with reference to its rites and ceremonies"

I guess we are!!

How do we keep it?

139

As long as the ties that bind us are stronger

than those that will tear us apart,

all will be well.

We keep what we have only with vigilance.

Who are these life-savers?

They are the angels in the rooms.

We are all children of God.

Sweet Tooth

Popcorn and ice cream

Coffee and cream.

I like to dance and like to dream.

I got a sweet tooth and it's all mine.

Gotta have the good stuff, so divine!

Friday I'll make you

a marshmallow pie.

You'll eat it right up

straight in front of my eyes.

Inside I will want to die

because I had to kiss sweets

goodbye!

Tomorrow I'll look you

straight in the eye.

And tell you simply why,

when I look at

fruit cake, chocolate and pie

I just want to cry.

141

So yummy but no, I can't touch.

The stuffs so good I want too much.

Gained 15 pounds in this 12-step recovery,

what an unfortunate, wicked discovery!

Time and again

you pretend to be my friend.

But were never there

for my rock bottom end.

How can I trust

my vicious sugar lust.

Pancakes and maple syrup

Muffins and eggs.

I like to eat

and I like my feet.

So remind me again why I can't

have more treats?

A Prayer for the Sick and Suffering

Rub your eyes. Breath. Awaken.

It's a new day.

Let god's light shine upon your face.

Let the wisdom of knowing you are loved,

find you when the walls are closing in.

You are not alone.

Let the grace of youth so gay,

remind you what it's like to play.

If the simple things in life are free,

and life's a fleeting glimpse,

why not live to give?

Let go. Reach out and give a smile!

143

Ace of Spades

Ace of spades, like the card in poker everyone needs.

Ace of spades can also be low, lowest in fact where face cards feed.

But I'm on top today, alive and well-

Thanks to the dealer's magic spell.

Threw away those dirty razor blades and pill crushers.

So much for low ace button busters.

No more cutting.

No more sniffing.

No more pain.

But if the poker dealer cheats,

I got you beat-

I'll never tell the old sage.

Ace of spades, full of rage.

Never forget to thank the universe

for its untimely gifts.

No, no, not today.

Living clean and in the moment

is where it's at.

Cleaning out my closet

I forgot to sweep the floor.

People stare and I get lost in the glare-

Limelight.

Not where I like to be.

It's the disease which frightens me.

It's holding on, so tight.

But I won't give up without a fight.

No more hiding

No more gloom.

Ace of spades, you're on top-

You're ahead of the doom!

Threw away fortune and fame,

To give yourself a better name!

Frozen in a time capsule

of distant memories,

my bubble bursts as our eyes meet.

Settled in my mind, I peel away my disguise.

The pattern exists when more than your ego connects the dots.

Standing alone, only drifting from my center,

I glide towards another being only to convince myself I'm whole.

Rewind to moments of joy and laughter.

God was my friend.

Reflecting on past burdens we carry.

God was my guardian.

Flashes of pain, heart-ache and depression.

God was my salvation.

The journey has been one of great triumphs through desperate struggles.

With God's light shinning on my back, always ready to catch me when I fall.

Now, he walks beside me when I quiet my mind and accept the gift of the present.

Many Voices, Same Moon

Bravery Ails the Beautiful

Bravery is an iron fist harnessed by prayer shawls and placid faces.

In the sea of distraction, the oars man sets sail for another lone day.

On days when no one is watching.

No one is there to judge him.

He stands tall and suitably proud.

Bravery is a constant battle among thieves, witches and hungry vultures.

But in this great land of the free, only the strong will triumph.

Only then will beauty unfold...

Truth lies in the secretion of thought...

Drifters take a back seat and relax.

Listen to the sound of an empty cup.

Feel the vibrations of a beating heart.

As your wonder grows,

Beauty unfolds...

like Glenn Gould, feeling every key with precision and exuberance,

you become alive, joyous and free.

Centered for all of the world to see

what a blessing it is just to *be*.

The Healing Power of the Universe

Respect comes to those who give back.

The earth, all she does is give,

yet we continue to take.

While the universe, so vast

holds unfathomable answers

to the mysteries of our past.

We are so small in contextual reference,

so be good to our mother,

for she is our protector, our one true provider.

Still, when we cannot see,

let her powers heal the scars

mankind has placed

upon our wretched, weary faces.

School Life

Teaching is what I like to do.

Listen to the children.

They will show you where to go.

Inspire through joy and endless passion.

When in school, I never feel blue-

cause reaching out, it's all for you.

I hear your cry from time to time,

but no matter what, I'll never be far-

I'll never let up.

Time passes by and then you're surprised,

when you've opened a parachute mind.

Some hide behind a mask,

suppressing laughter, heart and soul-

surrendering to a nosy hole.

inner beauty lost and sold.

But no, not you, for you stand tall.

We catch each other each time we fall.

No robot space time for us at all.

We awaken the mind, body and soul.

Teaching is what I like to do.

Just When

Just when you thought you've accomplished some crafts-

the Buddha mind laughs.

Already you're unraveling your first big error-

stitches going "bye-bye" on your hand knit blanket.

Just when you thought you did the right thing

through truth & honesty-

you find out your truth telling got a man testy,

which in turn made him act out hasty.

Shot a guy on the grid. Now he's dead.

It'd have been safer if he was misled.

Just when you thought you made a good decision

based on an inner vision you held so tight,

choosing to walk away from the fight.

So the guy instead ended up in a brawl,

right outside with your best friend, Paul!

Just when you thought the perfect job was right around the
corner-

SNAP! You trip on a bulging tree root and bust your knee cap.

Now you're back in that medicine room

feeling like crap.

It's like a destiny trap!

no future planning...

no looking back...

Just this moment.

How long will it last?

I'm not sure, just don't let it pass.

Say hello with a kiss-

holding onto this state of nirvana

and ultimate bliss!

Zen Rock

Zen rock.

Zen roll.

Zen rock and roll.

Melodic fusion of an alternative groove.

Stars sparkle.

Stars dance.

Stars sparkle and dance.

Speaking their truths through gathered up
dreams & wishes.

Sun shines.

Sun blinds.

Sun shines and blinds.

Radiating rhyme schemes piercing the eyes.

I'm Fine

I'm fine. She says, so

alone and out in the cold.

Money just sits as

the future takes hold.

The banks took it all as

the married grow old.

I'm fine. She says, into

the luminous night sky.

Reflections of visions from

the lone passersby.

Waves move us along-

we stay close and nearby.

I'm fine. She says, as

illusions flood the streets.

Pushers and shovers creep-

forcing the young to retreat-

once again in defeat.

Clouded Memories

Alone in the zone

he sits back in his throne-

reflecting on the past

where he buried his bone.

Lost in old memories so shady-

like a raving Marsha Brady.

Chaos waits behind the reddish curtain-

where Navy boy Johnny's been bruised and hurtin'.

March: Spring Around the Corner

Snow, grimy

Ice, melting

Spring around the corner

Faces still welting.

Darkness, fading

Children, laughing

Diseases on exodus

Still at times, baffling.

Music, dancing

Fire, burning

Desires grow deep

and his wheels are turning!

Passion, dramatic

Fire, burning

On the threshold

She exhales a yearning

Pondering...

    Waiting...

        Anticipating...

Voices, echo

Fragile, deceptive

Not a moment too late-

rented space in a single perspective.

Fate...

    Destiny...

        Life's design...

Shallow in cries

And lonely lullabies-

don't forget to kiss

mommy goodbye.

Home, safe

Rent, due

Lost in space

159

What's a girl to do?

Guess I'll just let it be.

No need to foresee

what's just around the corner,

waiting to...

or

waiting till... Spring.

Lifestyles

Mountains of crisp green and many trees.

acres and acres of undisturbed grass.

Is the dollar so powerful that

we've chosen to leave this all behind?

Extraordinary mansions, shops and highways

block this gorgeous view.

Yet if you drive far enough away from it all

you might catch a glimpse and maybe you'll fall-

in love with nature like I have.

In these parts we cry.

Did we choose to live this way?

or did we just evolve?

Unstoppable destruction, no doubt-

will lead us to our final demise.

Tick-Tock there goes the clock.

Time is wasted on wars brewing

and anarchy stirring.

We sabotaged our one true cause

and must never forget,

the way we live out lifestyles,

is how we end up with regrets.

The Musical Magician's Mystery

When we crawl up from the magician's
white rabbit's fur,
try as we must to figure out life's unsolved mysteries,
we see it in the depth of the artist's soul,
reflected through charcoal sketches,
shadowy figures and acrylic designs.
We see it in the poet, what's in between the lines...
We see it in our historical heroes,
The Shakespeare's, Van-Gogh's, Dali's and Thoreaus...
In a child's first snowmen and a baby's first words.
So brilliant and beautiful, the blank slate
inside our mind
allowing us to create, discover and explore all
different finds.
We see it in the way we hear an unforgettable musical
score like
Star Wars, ET, American Beauty, or even Cheers, True Blood or
Dexter.
Or when you hear a piece for the first time and can't stop
listening.

163

So when you're feeling sad and blue-

Listen to your heart.

You'll know what to do.

Snow Tide

Gray - faded, color -wrinkled

leaves buried under mounds of snow.

Slowly falling flakes dancing

gracefully upon their descent.

Each textured flake unique

And oh so sleek.

"Oh so beautiful" sang the man on his knees

to the barren trees.

Every last remnant of fall is gone-

Ice from the storm glimmers off the tree limbs.

Beauty and grace

mask their

disheveled

naked

figures,

emerging taller

sturdier-

and oh so bright.

Images of winter reflected through the child-eyes of blue...

Through icicles glittered brown specks of

whites, golds and silvers too...

My soul cries out in pure delight.

Never before have I seen

such a magnificent sight.

Tide comes in strong

in the form of wind and sleet-

As if in vision while in sleep.

How does one explain what can only be seen

by tired eyes and a tarnished soul?

Passing on slowly-

I have no regrets.

Slush, slush...

Mush, mush...

Boots splashing in muddy puddles.

Walking on...

Standing tall...

Steps of pride...

I'll never forget the obsolete beauty

of the snow tide.

How lucky for a tarnished soul-to be forgiven

by the divine

then given

the gift of tranquil eyes

to see beyond societal designs

of misery and cries.

Snow tide.

Grace, my God, the universe,

I thank you for the eyes to see

through the ego masked over me.

The Impermanence of Snow

<<Stretch, yawn, smile>>

Rising out of bed.

Oh dread.

Can't see through the window sill.

Another day to plow, grip and just sit still.

Don't think of taking another pill.

Your schedule is shot.

Your motivation rot.

There's only one way to fix this aching need.

Hit the sheet and go back to sleep.

It's a snow day!

I should be happy, but I'm not.

There's been too many days I fought-

to keep my sanity in check

but it's easy to forget,

when everything outside is wet.

Many Voices, One Moon

Many voices, one moon...

Look to the sky

when yearning to cry.

We are all just pieces of the same puzzle.

We must keep this in mind before we act rash in a hustle.

The curse may be lifted, we can unlatch our muzzles.

Speak up. Speak out. Speak close. Speak far.

Speak the truth wherever you are.

Many voices, one moon...

Remember, we share the same stars.

Release the chains that bind you.

Too familiar? Too comforting?

Maybe.

But exciting? Inspiring? Enlightening?

No.

So don't be afraid to break through,

or hold back.

Be all that is you.

We are all pieces of the same puzzle.

To be here, is to be home.

169

So be *here* or bust!

Make the choice fast before it no longer lasts.

Why are you scared?

If it the ghosts of your past?

Well, no worries, then-

It's not yours to hold on to.

Let go of the ego that engages you.

It's nothing more than tears and sorrow.

Enjoy the moments of today,

for you may not always have tomorrow.

10885417R00097

Made in the USA
Charleston, SC
12 January 2012